Meet Our New Student From GREAT BRITAIN

Tamra Orr

Mitchell Lane
PUBLISHERS

P.O. Box 196
Hockessin, Delaware 19707
Visit us on the web: www.mitchelllane.com
Comments? email us: mitchelllane@mitchelllane.com

Meet Our New Student From

Australia • China • Colombia • **Great Britain**
• Haiti • Israel • Korea • Malaysia • Mexico
• New Zealand • Nigeria • Tanzania

Library of Congress Cataloging-in Publication Data

Orr, Tamra.
  Meet our new student from Great Britain / by Tamra Orr.
      p. cm.—(A Robbie reader)
  Includes bibliographical references and index.
  ISBN 978-1-58415-648-2 (lib. bdg.)
  1. Great Britain—Juvenile literature. I. Title.
  DA27.5.O77 2008
  941—dc22
                                                2008002270

Printing   1   2   3   4   5   6   7   8   9

                                                        PLB

CONTENTS

Great Britain

The Clock Tower in London is often called Big Ben. That is actually the name of the bell inside the four-faced clock at the top of the tower. Big Ben's official name is the Great Bell.

Big News

Chapter 1

As soon as I walked into class, I knew something was different. Everyone did. One look at Mrs. South's face and we knew. She had a secret! We could not wait for her to tell us. Everyone was whispering about it.

She started the day like she always did. She read off each of our names to see if we were there.

"Ellen Winters?"

"Here."

"Colin Wyatt?"

"Yes, Mrs. South."

"Jennifer Young? . . . Jennifer Young?"

"Oh, here!" I said. I had been so busy thinking about the secret that I had almost missed my own name.

After Mrs. South was finished taking roll, she looked up and smiled. We knew the moment had come. She was going to tell us something exciting.

Caernarfon Castle in Gwynedd, Wales, was built between 1283 and 1327 by Edward I. At this castle in 1301, his son, Prince Edward, was given the title Prince of Wales. Since then, every firstborn son of the monarchy has been called the Prince of Wales.

"Our class is getting a new student next week," said Mrs. South. "His name is Michael Hammond."

Some of the students started to whisper again. I could tell they were a little disappointed. I was too. Jefferson Elementary School had gotten four new students this year already. It was fun, but it was nothing unusual.

"Oh, wait. Did I tell you that Michael is from another country?" Mrs. South asked, with a smile.

"Where?" asked Kwan.

"Does he speak English?" asked Natalia.

"What kind of clothes does he wear?" asked Julio.

"He is from Great Britain," explained Mrs. South. "Does anyone know where that is?"

I held up my hand. "Isn't that another name for England?" I asked.

"You are partly right," replied Mrs. South. "Great Britain does include England. It also includes Scotland and Wales. Along with Northern Ireland, it

British Guard

Sheep are raised in many parts of Great Britain. Clothing is made from the wool in their thick coats, and their meat is common in British foods.

is part of the United Kingdom of Great Britain and Northern Ireland, or the UK."

"It sounds big," said Jacob.

"It does—but it isn't," explained Mrs. South. She pulled a world map down from the left wall of the classroom. "Here it is," she said, pointing to a small place in Europe. "It is less than a third the size of Texas."

Where in the World

Outer Hebrides
Inner Hebrides
Highlands

ATLANTIC
OCEAN

Edinburgh
Glasgow
SCOTLAND

NORTHERN IRELAND
Belfast

Dublin
Irish
Sea

EIRE

York

Liverpool

Nottingham

WALES

ENGLAND

Bristol
Cardiff
London
Southampton
Dover

English Channel

Channel
Islands

FRANCE

FACTS ABOUT THE UNITED KINGDOM

UK Total Area:
94,525 square miles
(244,820 square kilometers)

Population:
60 million (2007)

Capital City:
London

Religions:
Christian (Roman Catholic and
Protestant), Muslim, Sikh, Hindu, Jewish

Languages:
English (official language);
Welsh; Gaelic

Chief Exports:
Manufactured goods, fuels, chemicals,
food, beverages, and tobacco

Monetary Unit:
Pound sterling (£); one pound equals
100 pence

Westminster Abbey is part of the Church of England. Since 1066, kings and queens have been crowned there. For over 1400 years, church services have been held every day in Westminster Abbey.

The choir sits in the rows of seats along an aisle in Westminster Abbey. Aside from the living worshipers, there are more than 3,300 people buried in the abbey, including royalty and famous authors, artists, and scientists.

"What language does he speak?" asked Lilly. "I mean, we speak English, so what about him?"

"Michael speaks English also, Lilly. He will say things a little differently than we do, though. He also uses different words than we do for some things. Before he gets here, we will learn some of those words."

Mrs. South walked over to the chalkboard. "In fact," she added, "we are going to learn a lot about Great Britain before Michael arrives. I want him to feel

British coin

welcome, so we will learn about his country. We will also make a craft for him to enjoy when he gets here. The morning he comes to class, we will even serve a special snack that comes from his country."

I smiled. This was going to be a great week. First, we

Cricket is a popular game in many parts of Great Britain. Players, usually dressed in white, use a bat to try to hit a fist-sized ball through wickets.

Buckingham Palace, with its 775 rooms, is the official home of the queen of England. It is the setting for state occasions and royal entertaining, and it is open to tourists.

would learn about a new place and spend extra time doing art, and then Monday, we would get to meet a new person. Best of all, we would get something good to eat! This was Mrs. South's best surprise ever.

Great Britain

Stonehenge is a monument found in the county of Wiltshire, near Salisbury, England. It was built over hundreds of years, beginning more than 5,000 years ago. Scientists believe it was used in ancient religious ceremonies.

A Look Back
Through Time

Chapter

The history of Great Britain spans thousands of years. There have been people in the area since the first Stone Age hunters came through more than 500,000 years ago. It wasn't until the year 3000 BCE that people from other parts of Europe began to move in. They cut down forests. Many became farmers and planted crops. In 500 BCE, they were joined by the Celts (KELTS), who brought iron tools. The Celts were a warlike people who fought against the people of Britain and other tribes to take control of the land.

One sign that people lived there thousands of years ago is Stonehenge, a famous group of standing stones in south England. Experts believe it was built about 2000 BCE. What were these big rocks for? No one is sure. Most researchers think they were used to measure the movements of the sun and the moon. How did people make something like this so long ago? That is a mystery that no one has been able to figure out yet.

For many years, Britain was attacked again and again. In 55 CE, the Romans came, led by Julius Caesar. They did not stay long but returned in 43 CE to invade once again. This time they won. Britain became a part of the Roman Empire. Just over 27 years later, the Romans also conquered Wales. Seventy years later, Rome took over Scotland. In 401 CE, the Anglo-Saxons from Germany took over. They were followed by the Vikings from Scandinavia (what is now Norway and Denmark). In 1066, the Normans from France conquered King Harold. They ruled the island for centuries. By the end of the Middle Ages (1450–1500), their king also ruled Wales and Ireland.

By 1603, England and Scotland had the same king. King James called himself the King of Great Britain. However, "Great Britain" would not be an official country until 1707.

When James took the throne, all was not well. A growing number of merchants and noblemen known as **parliament** (PAR-luh-ment) did not like the way the country was being ruled. They demanded a change. In the 1640s, the demand turned into a war. The people won! Now they could elect their leaders rather than just accept whoever inherited the position.

If the people overthrew the king, why does the country still have a queen and prince? The royal

THE BRITISH EMPIRE in 1914

Lands in the
British Empire

GREAT BRITAIN

ASIA

INDIA

AFRICA

AUSTRALIA

NEW
ZEALAND

CANADA

UNITED STATES
OF AMERICA

SOUTH
AMERICA

At its peak in 1914, the British Empire was the largest empire in history. It controlled territory in North America, South America, Africa, Asia (including all of India), Australia, and New Zealand.

family was allowed to stay in their palaces (including Buckingham Palace and Windsor Palace), but they have limited power in the country's government. The leader is the country's **prime minister** instead.

In 1801, England, Scotland, and Wales, along with the province of Northern Ireland, formed the United Kingdom of Great Britain and Northern Ireland, or simply the United Kingdom, or UK.

Most of Ireland became independent from the United Kingdom in 1921. That part is now called the Irish Republic, or Eire. Northern Ireland remains part of the UK.

Many things changed when World War I started in 1914. Germany invaded a country called Belgium. Great Britain was sworn to protect Belgium, so it had to get involved in the war. Although Great Britain was on the winning side of the war, the victory was costly. Great Britain lost many men and lots of money.

Like people in the United States, the British struggled through the hard times of the 1920s and 1930s. Money and jobs were hard to find. Life got

Pentre Ifan (meaning "Ivan's home") has been standing in Wales since at least 4000 BCE. This megalith, or gathering of large stones, marks a burial ground. Experts think the stones weigh more than 40 tons.

harder in 1939 when World War II began. Again, Great Britain lost thousands of men, and millions of dollars in property was damaged.

Great Britain has grown and changed since the 1940s. In the early 2000s, it was one of America's biggest **allies**. Queen Elizabeth II is still a powerful symbol of England, as is her son, Prince Charles. Prime Minister Tony Blair stepped down in 2007 and was replaced by Gordon Brown.

Great Britain

Trafalgar Square in the heart of London reminds people of the Battle of Trafalgar, fought in 1805. British naval hero Admiral Lord Nelson defeated a much larger French and Spanish fleet in the battle near Spain.

A Beautiful Land

Chapter **3**

Despite its name—and the fact that it includes England, Scotland, and Wales—Great Britain is not very large. Although it is the largest island in Europe, it is just over 88,000 square miles, which is smaller than the state of Oregon. If you look at a map (see the one on page 9), you can see that the English Channel is what separates Great Britain from France and the rest of Europe. North America and Great Britain are separated by the Atlantic Ocean.

A Walk Through England

England is known for its quiet countryside, but there's a lot more to it than that. Do you like big cities with lots of fun things to do? Go to London, the capital of England. Watch out for the traffic, though! In Great Britain, they drive on the opposite side of the road from Americans. Look inside one of the cars. The steering wheel is on the other side! Of course, you could always take a ride in one of London's double-deck buses.

Although much in London is very new and up to date, there is an older part. It is called The City. It has old ruins from Roman times, plus churches built back in the Middle Ages. There is even a 3,500-year-old stone called Cleopatra's Needle. It was given to England in 1819 by Egypt, where Cleopatra had been queen.

Much of the land outside London belongs to farmers, especially in the north and southeast. In the middle of England is the town of Nottingham, the setting for the Robin Hood stories.

fun FACTS

Scotland is the home of the legendary Lochness Monster, or Nessie, as she is called. People say they have seen her pop her dinosaur-like head up out of the water, but no one has ever been able to prove she is really there. Everyone keeps looking anyway!

Welcome to Scotland

Scotland is lush and green. There are fewer people in Scotland than in any other part of Great Britain. There, you can see nature at its best. You can also visit **moors**, which are boggy fields of scrubs and grass;

St. Michael's Mount in Cornwall is an island 500 yards from the mainland. When the tide is out, it is possible to walk to the mount. The castle was built in 1193. It has been used as both a church and a fortress.

Wembley Stadium in London is home to the England national soccer team. It can fit 90,000 people and is so tall, it has an aircraft warning beacon on it.

the Highlands, or mountainous region; **glens** (valleys); and **lochs** (lakes). There are also some large cities, like Glasgow (GLAS-goh) and Edinburgh (which you might think is pronounced EE-din-burg, but is actually pronounced EH-din-bur-ah). Many Scots are huge soccer fans. They love to watch their favorite players on the pitch (field). They love music too, and the sounds of drums and bagpipes are familiar ones.

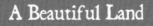

On into Wales

At just over 8,000 square miles, Wales is small, but still home to about three million Welsh. Most of the people live in the valleys and places along the coast in the

Flag of Wales

south. The largest city is Cardiff. In Wales, the people tend to speak Welsh instead of English, and their street and store signs are often written in both languages.

Wales has more than a dozen mountains that soar over 3,000 feet into the sky. It also has long stretches of sandy beaches. More than three-fourths of the land is used for farming and raising livestock.

Snowdon Peak in northern Wales is one of the highest mountains in Great Britain. There are trails on all sides of it for everyone from the beginner to the advanced climber. A 10-mile footrace is held on its slopes every year.

A train station in Wales welcomes visitors by helping them pronounce the name of the town.

A village in Wales holds the record for the longest name in the whole world. It is called **Llanfairpwllgwyngyllgogerychwyrndrobwllllantysiliogogogoch**. What does it mean? "St. Mary's Church in a hollow of the white hazel near to the rapid whirlpool and St. Tysilio's Church of the red cave."

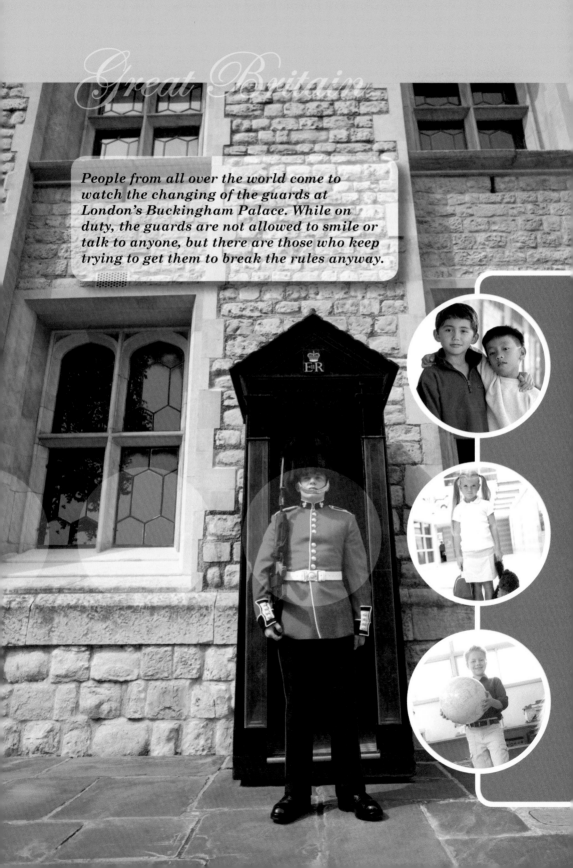

People from all over the world come to watch the changing of the guards at London's Buckingham Palace. While on duty, the guards are not allowed to smile or talk to anyone, but there are those who keep trying to get them to break the rules anyway.

A Country of Tradition

Chapter 4

When people think of Great Britain, a number of things come to mind. One of them is tea. Another is rain. Both of them are very common throughout Great Britain.

Time to Eat!

Hot tea is one of the most popular drinks in the United Kingdom. In fact, the people there (about 60 million) drink more than 200 million cups of tea every day! A lot of them have "afternoon tea" about 4:00 P.M. This is a mid-afternoon time to sit down and have a spot of hot tea with some kind of sweet snack like cookies and cake or sometimes a simple sandwich. The tea is usually prepared in a special china teapot. Instead of tea bags, many people use tea leaves. Milk is often added for just the right taste.

While the Brits eat a lot of the same foods as Americans do, there are certain dishes that are considered to be British. For example, fish and chips

Fish and chips has been a popular British dish since the middle 1800s. It is sold in fish-and-chip shops called chippies.

is a favorite meal. The fish is fried, and the chips are actually french fries. Another favorite is steak and kidney pie, which is meat cooked in a pastry shell. Yorkshire pudding—crisp, hollow rolls baked in beef fat—is a common side dish. It is served with roast beef and potatoes.

In Scotland, a traditional meal is haggis. It is often served on St. Andrew's Day (November 30, Scotland's national holiday) and on Burns Night (September 25), which celebrates Scottish poet Robert Burns. Haggis is a mixture of oatmeal and sheep lungs, heart, liver, and kidney, cooked in the sheep's stomach lining. On Burns Night, as Burns's poem "Ode to a Haggis" is recited, the dish is sliced open and served.

How Is the Weather?
Great Britain is known for its tea drinking—and for its rainy weather. It gets a lot of rain because it is surrounded by water. The whole area has cool

High tea is an important part of life in Great Britain. It is taken seriously, and often only the best dishes in the house are used for this light meal.

British coins are counted in pence, and bills are counted in pounds sterling. The queen is on many pieces of British money. Since the 1990s, the government has considered switching its currency to the euro, which is used by many other European countries.

summers and mild winters. London's summers rarely go over 64 degrees Fahrenheit, and winters do not drop below 40 degrees. Wales is quite similar, but Scotland is cooler. Great Britain averages 27 to 150 inches of rain each year, depending on the area.

Meet the People

More than three-fourths of the people in Great Britain are from England. About 10 percent are Scottish. The rest are a combination of Welsh and groups of people

fun FACTS

One of the best-known bands in music history is the Beatles. The group was made up of Paul McCartney, John Lennon, George Harrison, and Ringo Starr. They recorded their first album in 1963, and before long, they had the top five spots on the Billboard Chart. No other group has ever been able to do that. After recording many very popular albums, they broke up in 1970. By 2001, two of the band members had died.

from places like India, Pakistan, Africa, and China.

Many famous authors created some of the most amazing characters in Great Britain. A. A. Milne's Winnie the Pooh lived in the One Hundred Acre Woods, and Lewis Carroll introduced Alice in Wonderland. Sir Arthur Conan Doyle, who was Scottish, set his Sherlock Holmes mysteries in England. And William Shakespeare wrote countless stage plays in London. J.R.R. Tolkien created hobbits and elves, and J.K. Rowling wrote seven books about the adventures of Harry Potter and Hogwarts.

Other famous people from Great Britain include singers David Bowie, Mick Jagger and the Rolling Stones, and legendary rockers the Beatles. Popular singer Joss Stone is from England, as well as the group Muse. Franz Ferdinand is a Scottish group.

Schoolchildren in the UK get a lesson on bagpipes. This wind instrument has been around for hundreds of years. It was a popular instrument for dance, and is still used by police forces and the military.

Soccer star David Beckham is also from England, along with Sir Steve Redgrave, gold medalist rower.

A School Day

School in Great Britain is a lot like school in the United States, but there are some differences. The year is 39 weeks long and is divided into six terms. Students get a Christmas vacation, plus a spring and summer break. Most schools require uniforms. Boys wear gray or black pants, a white shirt, a tie, and a sweater. Girls wear the same thing, except the pants are replaced by skirts.

Although Great Britain's schools are different, the kids are quite the same. They enjoy making friends, playing games, and learning about the world in which they live.

Great Britain

Michael told us about a park near his house in York. People can picnic on the grass next to the ruins of an old church.

A Spot of Tea and Union Jack

Chapter 5

On Monday morning, Mrs. South did not even need to take attendance. It was clear that everyone was there. No one wanted to miss meeting Michael. Our craft was ready to make. Our snack was ready to eat. We had learned all about Great Britain's history, geography, religions, weather, and holidays. We studied the town of York most, since that is where Michael was from. We had listened to music by the Beatles. We had even read about Queen Elizabeth and Prince Charles. We were ready!

When Michael came into the room, I was surprised. He did not look any different from the other boys in my class. He was very quiet. I did not blame him. It must be hard to leave the place you know and go someplace far away, where everyone is a stranger.

"Welcome to Jefferson Elementary, Michael," said Mrs. South. "Your desk is right over here."

The United States has always had close ties with Great Britain. The red and white stripes on the American flag stand for the thirteen British colonies in North America. After the United States became independent from Great Britain, the two countries became allies.

Michael went horseback riding last year on Boxing Day. In England, Boxing Day is celebrated on December 26, the day after Christmas. It is a day to give to the less fortunate. Traditionally, it has also been a day to go foxhunting, a sport that involves chasing a fox on horseback. Since 2004, the rules for foxhunting have changed in an effort to protect the foxes, but people still go for the ride.

Michael smiled when he saw that we had put a Union Jack flag on his desk. "Thanks, mates," he said softly. I smiled at him. *Mates* sounded much more interesting than *friends*.

"We have a snack for you, Michael," said Mrs. South. "We thought you might like a cup of tea and some biscuits. We have been reading about food where you live, and tea seemed like something almost everyone in Great Britain likes."

Maria and Jeffrey carefully carried cups of tea to each student in the class. While everyone snacked on "biscuits" (cookies) and sipped on tea, they asked Michael a lot of questions.

I liked the way Michael talked. He used mostly the same words as I did, but they sounded different when he said them.

"We've been learning some of the words you use in Great Britain, and they're pretty neat," I said to Michael. "We made a list of them on the board."

Michael looked at the list and smiled. It read:

AMERICAN = BRITISH	AMERICAN = BRITISH
trunk = boot	truck = lorry
umbrella = brolly	gasoline = petrol
goodbye = cheerio	subway = underground
apartment = flat	flashlight = torch
elevator = lift	a difficult situation = a
stroller = pram	sticky wicket

"I never thought about that before," he admitted. "We do have some different words, don't we?"

I nodded at him. "I like yours better," I said.

He grinned. "Funny—I like yours!"

I laughed. I had an idea that Michael would have no trouble fitting in here and finding a lot of new mates. He already had one in me!

How To Make
Welsh Rarebit

This dish is also called Welsh rabbit—but there's no bunny involved!

Instructions

1. **With the help of an adult,** heat the butter in a pan on the stove.
2. Add the milk, cheese, mustard, and spices.
3. Stir until the cheese is melted.
4. Pour the mix over the toast.
5. Serve quickly and eat!

You Will Need

Pan

Spoon

Toaster

An adult to help you

Ingredients

1 ounce butter

2 teaspoons milk

4 ounces grated cheddar cheese

1 teaspoon mustard

Any spice you like (salt, pepper, garlic, onion powder, etc.)

4 pieces of hot, buttered toast

Make Your Own
Union Jack

You Will Need

**Red, White, and Blue
Construction Paper**

Glue

Scissors

The Union Jack is the national flag of the United Kingdom of Great Britain and Northern Ireland. The red cross stands for England. The white diagonal cross on blue stands for Scotland. The narrower red diagonal cross over white stands for Ireland. (Wales has its own flag.)

Instructions For Making A Union Jack

Use a whole piece of blue construction paper as your background for the flag.

2 Cut two pieces of white paper to cross the blue diagonally.

3 Cut two narrower pieces of red to lay over the white. Glue the white and red pieces to the blue, as shown on the flag below.

4 Cut out a white cross to go over the white-and-red X.

5 Cut out a red cross that is a little narrower than the white cross. Center it over top of the white cross to leave a white outline. Glue the red cross to the white cross.

Further Reading

Books

Bradley, Michael. *Great Britain*. Tarrytown, New York: Marshall Cavendish, 2005.

Cawood, Ian. *Britain in the Twentieth Century*. New York: Routledge, 2003.

Flip Quiz Great Britain. Great Bardfield, Essex, England: Miles Kelly Publishing, 2001.

Gordon, Sharon. *Great Britain*. Tarrytown, New York: Benchmark Books, 2004.

Oliver, Clare. *Great Britain*. Danbury, Connecticut: Franklin Watts Publishing, 2006.

West, Mark. *Great Britain*. Lanham, Maryland: Scarecrow Press, 2003.

Works Consulted

Automobile Association of Britain. *Exploring Britain*. London: W.W. Norton and Company, 2001.

Hull, Lisa. *The Great Castles of Britain and Ireland*. London: New Holland Publishers, 2006.

Lacey, Robert. *Great Tales from English History: A Treasury of True Stories about the Extraordinary People Who Made Britain Great*. New York: Back Bay Books, 2007.

Morgan, Kenneth, ed. *The Oxford History of Britain*. London: Oxford University Press, 2001.

Thackeray, Frank, and John Finding. *Events That Changed Great Britain Since 1689*. Westport, Connecticut: Greenwood Press, 2002.

Cooks.com, "Welsh Rarebit" www.cooks.com/rec/doc/0,1626,148168-241195,00.html

National Archives, UK: Cleopatra's Needle http://yourarchives.nationalarchives.gov.uk/index. php?title=Cleopatra's_Needle

Further Reading

Project Britain: British Life and Customs
www.woodlands-junior.kent.sch.uk/customs/questions/food/
meals.htm

Great Britain: British History
http://www.great-britain.co.uk/history/history.htm

Union Jack: Union Flag of United Kingdom of Great Britain and
Northern Ireland
http://www.know-britain.com/general/union_jack.html

On the Internet

British Embassy 4Kids http://www.britainusa.com/4Kids

CIA World Factbook: United Kingdom
https://www.cia.gov/library/publications/
the-world-factbook/geos/uk.html

National Archives Learning Curve: The British Empire
http://www.learningcurve.gov.uk/empire/

Official Web Site of the British Monarchy
http://www.royal.gov.uk/output/Page1.asp

The United Kingdom or Great Britain?
http://www.geo.ed.ac.uk/home/scotland/britain.html

What Is Boxing Day in England?
http://www.woodlands-junior.kent.sch.uk/customs/Xmas/
boxingday.html

Embassy

The British Embassy
3100 Massachusetts Avenue NW
Washington, D.C. 20008-3600
http://www.britainusa.com/

Glossary

allies (AL-lyz)—Friends or groups of people on your side.

glens—British term for valleys.

lochs (LOKS)—British term for lakes.

monarchy (MAH-nar-kee)—The government or rule of a king or queen.

moors—British term for grass-covered hillsides.

parliament (PAR-luh-ment)—A group of people who make laws and govern a country.

prime minister (prym MIH-nih-ster)—The head of government in some countries, including Great Britain.

The Welsh corgi is a small breed of dog that originated in Wales. *Corgi* means "dwarf dog" in Welsh.

Index

ABOUT THE AUTHOR

Tamra Orr is the author of more than 120 nonfiction books for children of all ages. She has a bachelor's degree in secondary education and English, and has written for all the top national testing companies in the United States. She lives in the Pacific Northwest with her kids and husband. When Tamra was young, one of her favorite people in the world was from England. Ever since then, she has studied as much as she can about this fascinating country steeped in history.